CATS

Cat features

 Cats are possibly the most beautiful and graceful of all animals. They have fine fur which is often strikingly marked with spots or stripes, and elegant heads with pointed ears and large eyes. All cats are hunters that kill and eat their own food. A pet cat is one of the most popular of animal companions because it is affectionate, intelligent, and playful.

British tortoiseshell shorthair
The British tortoiseshell shorthair has short, stocky legs, with large round paws and a chunky body.

Ginger kitten
At four months old this kitten can rear up and balance on her hind legs.

Bright eyes
The bright yellow eyes and jet black fur of this British black shorthair prove that it is a purebred or pedigree cat.

Best buddies
Cats often show great affection for each other and can make long, lasting friendships.

Marmalade cat
This marmalade tabby kitten has thick marmalade-coloured fur with patches of white and a tabby-striped tail.

Black-and-white
The first bicolour longhairs were bred to look like black-and-white Dutch rabbits.

Oriental tortoiseshell
Cats pictured in Egyptian tombs had large, pointed ears with wedge-like faces, long noses and a square muzzle – just like this Oriental tortoiseshell.

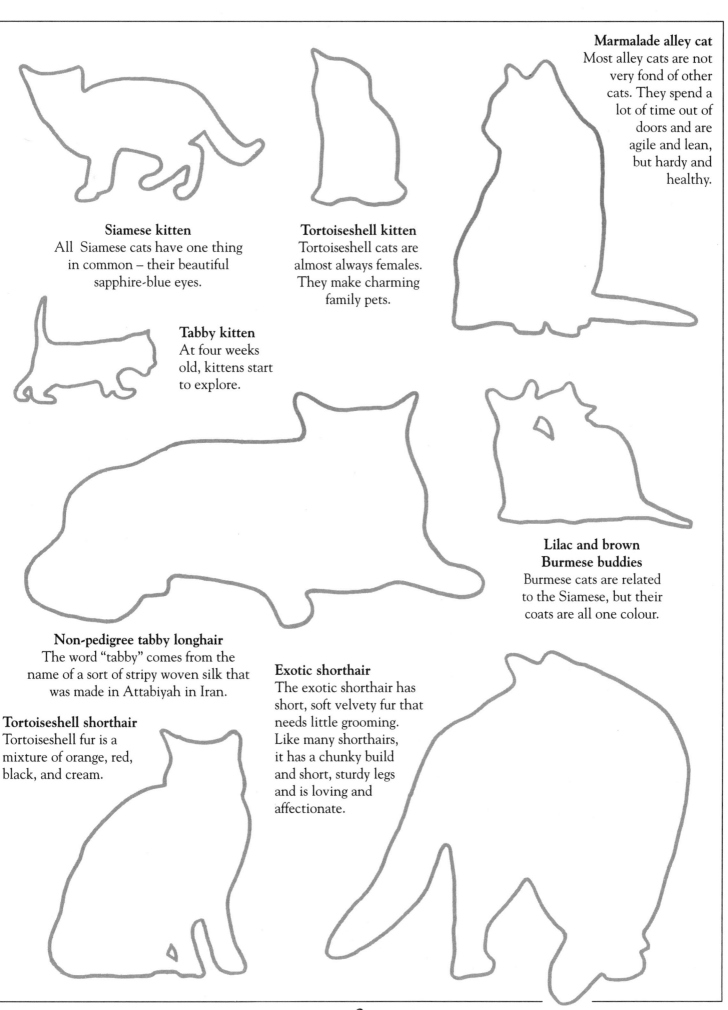

Marmalade alley cat
Most alley cats are not very fond of other cats. They spend a lot of time out of doors and are agile and lean, but hardy and healthy.

Siamese kitten
All Siamese cats have one thing in common – their beautiful sapphire-blue eyes.

Tortoiseshell kitten
Tortoiseshell cats are almost always females. They make charming family pets.

Tabby kitten
At four weeks old, kittens start to explore.

Lilac and brown Burmese buddies
Burmese cats are related to the Siamese, but their coats are all one colour.

Non-pedigree tabby longhair
The word "tabby" comes from the name of a sort of stripy woven silk that was made in Attabiyah in Iran.

Tortoiseshell shorthair
Tortoiseshell fur is a mixture of orange, red, black, and cream.

Exotic shorthair
The exotic shorthair has short, soft velvety fur that needs little grooming. Like many shorthairs, it has a chunky build and short, sturdy legs and is loving and affectionate.

A long thick coat

 Longhaired cats may have developed in cold countries like Russia where they would have needed a long, thick coat to protect them from the ice and snow of winter. Long hair takes a lot of grooming and can be a disadvantage because it becomes easily matted and gets caught and tangled in bushes. Longhaired cats usually have a gentle, friendly nature and are very popular pets.

Calico cat
In the USA, the blue tortoiseshell-and-white is known as the calico cat because its patched coat looks like a kind of cotton called calico.

Blue tortoiseshell-and-white longhair
This cat's thick, silky coat has patches of creamy ginger, blue, and white.

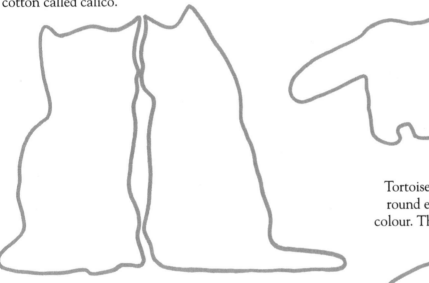

Tortoiseshell longhair
Tortoiseshell longhairs usually have big, round eyes of a lovely copper or orange colour. They make gentle and friendly pets.

Longhaired kittens
These two fluffy kittens may look adorable – but one day they will grow up. When looking for a pet, many people forget that grown-up longhairs need lots of attention, and their coats have to be groomed often.

Black longhair
With its long black coat and orange eyes, the black longhair is one of the oldest breeds. It dates back to the 16th century.

Tortie cameo longhair
If you carefully part this cat's fur, you can see an inner layer of short, fluffy white hairs and an outer coat of longer hairs with black, red, and cream tips.

Non-pedigree tabby longhair
This tabby has long hair, but is not a pedigree cat. This means it is a mixture of more than one breed.

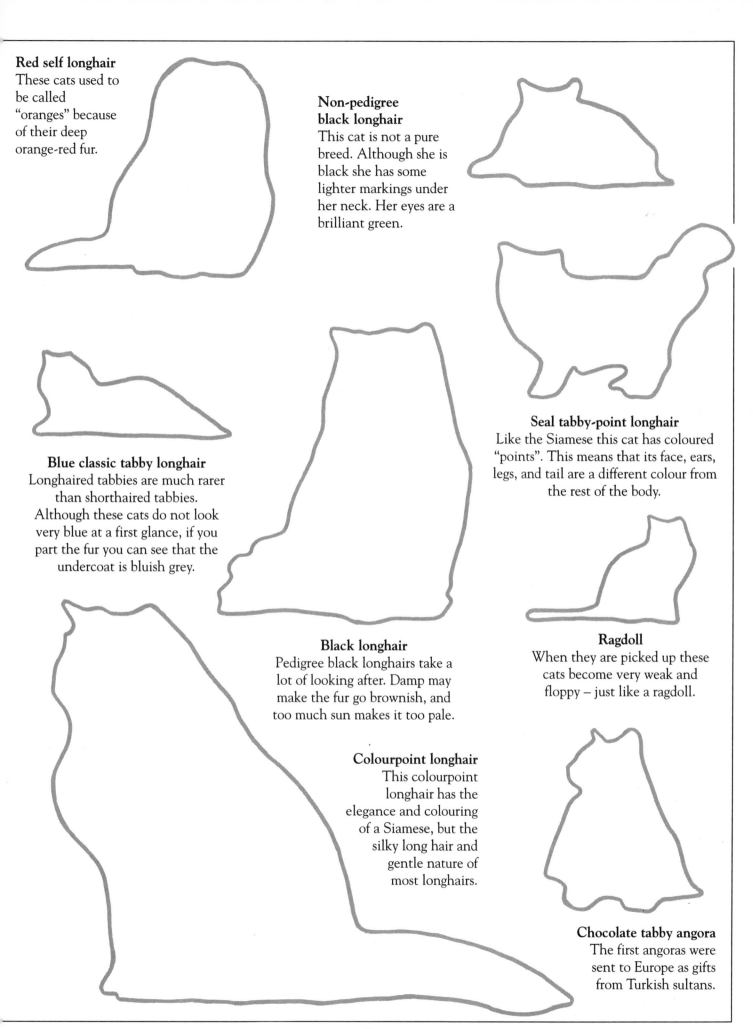

Red self longhair
These cats used to be called "oranges" because of their deep orange-red fur.

Non-pedigree black longhair
This cat is not a pure breed. Although she is black she has some lighter markings under her neck. Her eyes are a brilliant green.

Seal tabby-point longhair
Like the Siamese this cat has coloured "points". This means that its face, ears, legs, and tail are a different colour from the rest of the body.

Blue classic tabby longhair
Longhaired tabbies are much rarer than shorthaired tabbies. Although these cats do not look very blue at a first glance, if you part the fur you can see that the undercoat is bluish grey.

Black longhair
Pedigree black longhairs take a lot of looking after. Damp may make the fur go brownish, and too much sun makes it too pale.

Ragdoll
When they are picked up these cats become very weak and floppy – just like a ragdoll.

Colourpoint longhair
This colourpoint longhair has the elegance and colouring of a Siamese, but the silky long hair and gentle nature of most longhairs.

Chocolate tabby angora
The first angoras were sent to Europe as gifts from Turkish sultans.

Shorthaired cats

Shorthair tabby kitten
Many shorthair kittens have stripy tabby markings when they are very young.

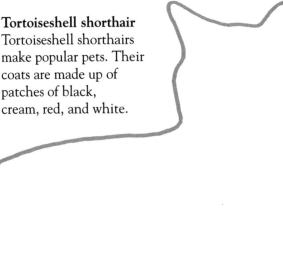

Shorthaired cats come in a wide variety of shapes, sizes and colours. Having a short coat makes it easier for a cat to survive and fend for itself. There is no danger of it becoming tangled in branches, or of enemies grabbing it, and shorthaired cats have less chance of getting skin diseases caused by matted fur. Pet shorthaired cats are easier to care for than their longhaired cousins as they need less grooming.

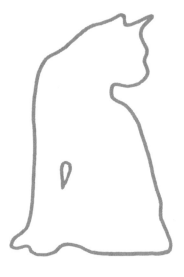

Down on the farm
This black-and-white shorthaired cat lives on a farm. It makes itself useful by catching mice in the farmyard.

British cream shorthair
This cat is a pedigree, or purebred shorthair. It has a short, thick tail and a stocky body.

White feet
This non-pedigree tortoiseshell-and-white shorthair looks to have four white socks.

Foreign blue shorthair
The foreign blue has a dark-grey coat with a distinct bluish tinge. The body is slim with long, slender legs and a tail that tapers down to a fine point.

Tortoiseshell shorthair
Tortoiseshell shorthairs make popular pets. Their coats are made up of patches of black, cream, red, and white.

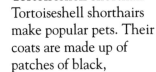

Chocolate cat
This chocolate Siamese tabby-point has sapphire-blue eyes and an ivory-coloured body with striped milk-chocolate points (ears, feet, and tail).

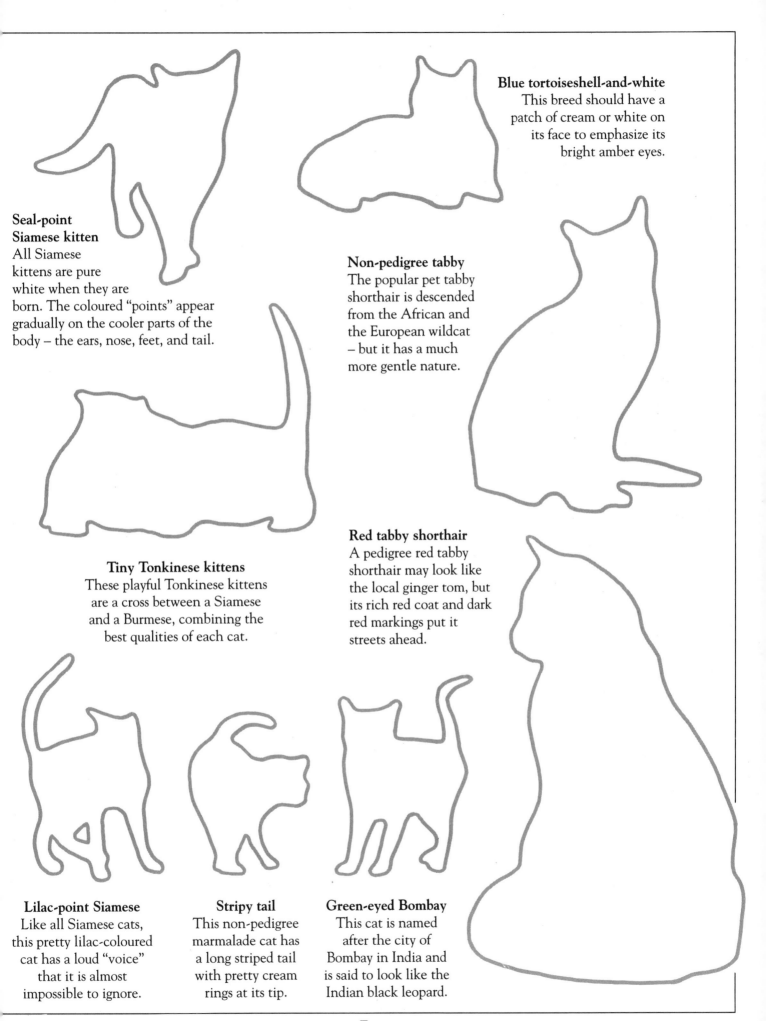

Seal-point Siamese kitten
All Siamese kittens are pure white when they are born. The coloured "points" appear gradually on the cooler parts of the body – the ears, nose, feet, and tail.

Blue tortoiseshell-and-white
This breed should have a patch of cream or white on its face to emphasize its bright amber eyes.

Non-pedigree tabby
The popular pet tabby shorthair is descended from the African and the European wildcat – but it has a much more gentle nature.

Tiny Tonkinese kittens
These playful Tonkinese kittens are a cross between a Siamese and a Burmese, combining the best qualities of each cat.

Red tabby shorthair
A pedigree red tabby shorthair may look like the local ginger tom, but its rich red coat and dark red markings put it streets ahead.

Lilac-point Siamese
Like all Siamese cats, this pretty lilac-coloured cat has a loud "voice" that it is almost impossible to ignore.

Stripy tail
This non-pedigree marmalade cat has a long striped tail with pretty cream rings at its tip.

Green-eyed Bombay
This cat is named after the city of Bombay in India and is said to look like the Indian black leopard.

7

Cat behaviour

 All cats behave in very similar ways whether they are big or little, wild cats or pets. They have a very keen sense of smell and from the moment they are born and before they can even see or hear, kittens can recognize their mother by her scent. Cats cannot talk to each other like humans, but they make noises such as chirruping a greeting or yowling. Cats sleep a lot, mostly during the day so they are ready to go out hunting at night-time.

Back off!
When a cat is scared or angry it arches its back, lowers its tail and all the hairs on its body stand on end.

A leaping pounce
To be a successful hunter a cat must be able to leap and pounce.

Learning to pounce
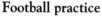
Kittens start learning to hunt almost as soon as they are born. This kitten is learning to pounce.

Stretching and rolling
Every so often a contented cat like this one will roll over or have a stretch before settling down to sleep again.

Football practice
Cats love to play football, but for them it is not a game. It is an opportunity to practise their hunting skills.

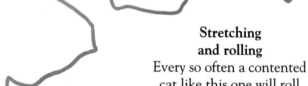

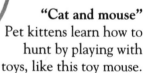

"Cat and mouse"
Pet kittens learn how to hunt by playing with toys, like this toy mouse.

Keeping clean
Kittens often wash each other as a way of making friends and getting to know their young brothers and sisters.

Cat napping
Cats often sleep during the day – ready to go out hunting at night.

DINOSAURS

Dinosaur defence

All dinosaurs needed to be able to defend themselves if they were attacked. Some dinosaurs were built for speed so they could run away from danger. But other dinosaurs had horns and claws and were often protected from head to toe by thick plates of body armour. Tails were often equipped with clubs or spikes, which the dinosaur could lash out at its enemies.

Baryonyx
This dinosaur's strong arms and enormous hooked claws were probably used for catching fish – but they could also be used against an attacker.

Rear and run
If in danger, the plant-eating *Scelidosaurus* would rear up on its tail – and run away.

Sordes
If the *Sordes* sensed danger, it would take to the air. It had small bones so it could fly away swiftly.

Formidable horn
Not many dinosaurs would dare attack the giant plant-eating *Eucentrosaurus*.

Spiky tail
Scolosaurus was well protected from attack. Its tail had two spikes at the end which the dinosaur used to knock over enemies.

Shonisaurus
This massive reptile of the seas had big paddles to swim away from danger.

Pachyrhinosaurus
This plant eater could defend itself with its spiky horn and bony neck frill.

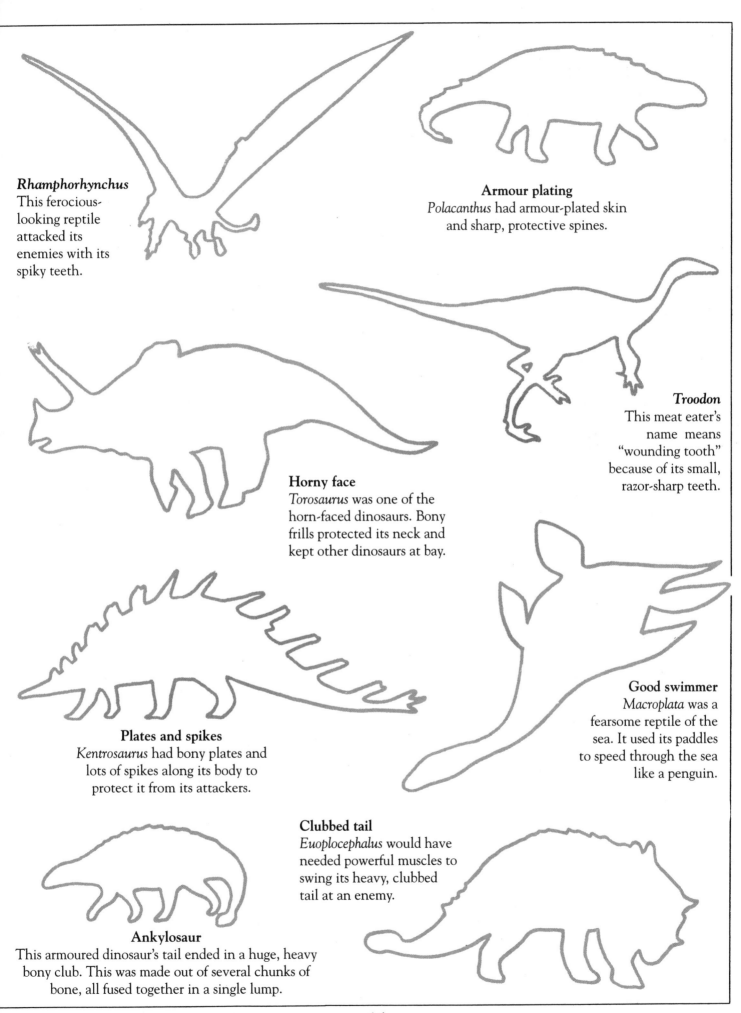

Rhamphorhynchus
This ferocious-looking reptile attacked its enemies with its spiky teeth.

Armour plating
Polacanthus had armour-plated skin and sharp, protective spines.

Troodon
This meat eater's name means "wounding tooth" because of its small, razor-sharp teeth.

Horny face
Torosaurus was one of the horn-faced dinosaurs. Bony frills protected its neck and kept other dinosaurs at bay.

Plates and spikes
Kentrosaurus had bony plates and lots of spikes along its body to protect it from its attackers.

Good swimmer
Macroplata was a fearsome reptile of the sea. It used its paddles to speed through the sea like a penguin.

Clubbed tail
Euoplocephalus would have needed powerful muscles to swing its heavy, clubbed tail at an enemy.

Ankylosaur
This armoured dinosaur's tail ended in a huge, heavy bony club. This was made out of several chunks of bone, all fused together in a single lump.

11

Funny faces

Some dinosaurs had unusual appearances such as funny-shaped heads, with lumps, crests, spikes, or helmets. Some of the most amazing heads belonged to the hadrosaurs, or "duck-billed dinosaurs", which had broad, toothless beaks. But oddly shaped heads had a purpose. Sometimes they attracted a mate or even scared off an enemy. A bony head could also be useful as a safety helmet, or to head-butt an enemy.

Long frills
Chasmosaurus was a long-frilled dinosaur and had a huge bony neck shield with a pointed horn on its nose and above each eye.

Egg head
Stegoceras had a knobbly, egg-shaped head. Rival males would have head-butting contests to win mates.

Balloon nose
Edmontosaurus was a duck-billed dinosaur. It had loose skin on its nose which it could blow up like a balloon.

Plain faced
Not all dinosaurs had funny faces. By comparison, *Iguanodon* looked quite plain. They were large, heavy plant eaters and probably walked on all fours.

Funny body, too!
Edmontonia was a large, heavily armoured plant eater that may have grown to a length of 7 m (23 ft).

Microceratops
This tiny plant eater was ony 76 cm (30 in) long. It had a horny beak and a small neck frill.

Crest head
Tsintaosaurus had a hollow, tubular crest that pointed upwards and forwards between the eyes.

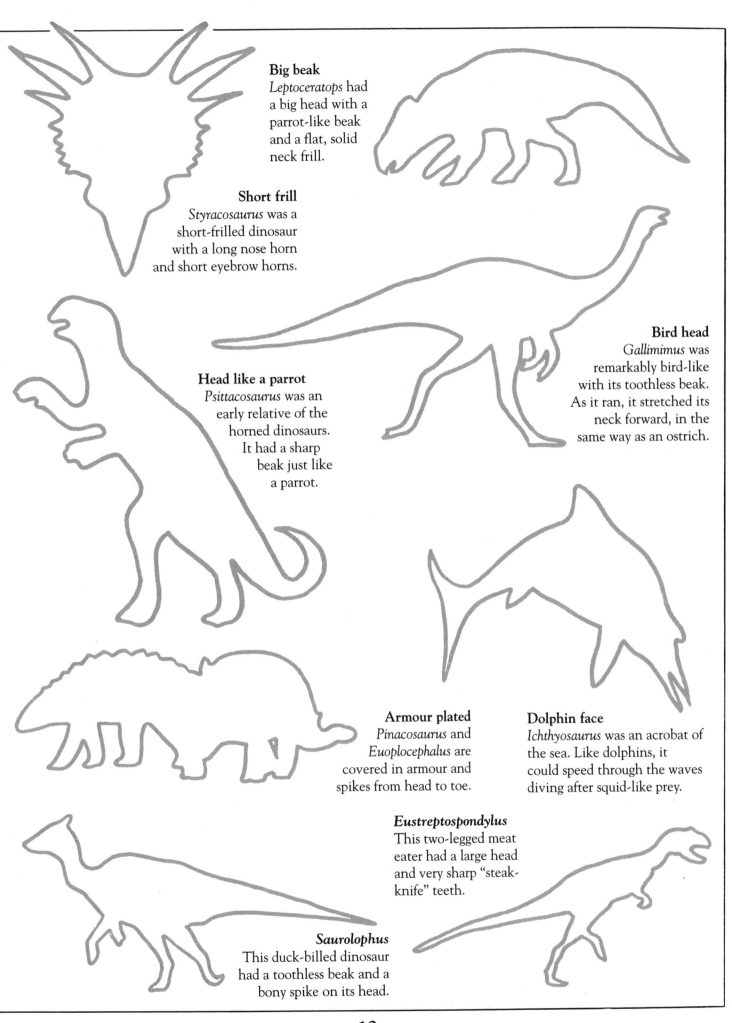

Big beak
Leptoceratops had a big head with a parrot-like beak and a flat, solid neck frill.

Short frill
Styracosaurus was a short-frilled dinosaur with a long nose horn and short eyebrow horns.

Head like a parrot
Psittacosaurus was an early relative of the horned dinosaurs. It had a sharp beak just like a parrot.

Bird head
Gallimimus was remarkably bird-like with its toothless beak. As it ran, it stretched its neck forward, in the same way as an ostrich.

Armour plated
Pinacosaurus and *Euoplocephalus* are covered in armour and spikes from head to toe.

Dolphin face
Ichthyosaurus was an acrobat of the sea. Like dolphins, it could speed through the waves diving after squid-like prey.

Eustreptospondylus
This two-legged meat eater had a large head and very sharp "steak-knife" teeth.

Saurolophus
This duck-billed dinosaur had a toothless beak and a bony spike on its head.

13

Around the world

Dinosaur remains have been found all over the world in every continent. The remains of the bones and teeth are found in rocks that formed when the dinosaurs were alive. Many countries have displays of dinosaur remains in their museums, and it is by studying these that we can learn more about these amazing creatures that ruled the world for 150 million years.

Brazilian pterosaur
Cearadactylus was a pterosaur. This Brazilian dinosaur flew on wings of skin that stretched from its body to the tips of its long fingers.

African stone-eater
Massospondylus, from southern Africa, did not have good teeth for eating plants. Instead, it swallowed stones which helped grind the plants in its stomach.

Velociraptor
This fast and fierce meat eater lived in China and Mongolia.

Australian vegetarian
The remains of *Muttaburrasaurus* were found in Australia. It was a large plant eater and walked on two feet.

Tiny Mongolian dinosaur
Bagaceratops was found in Mongolia. It was a tiny, horned dinosaur the size of a big dog.

North American dinosaur
Parasaurolophus came from North America. It had a long, hollow crest on its skull and a toothless beak.

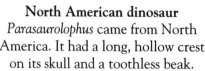

14

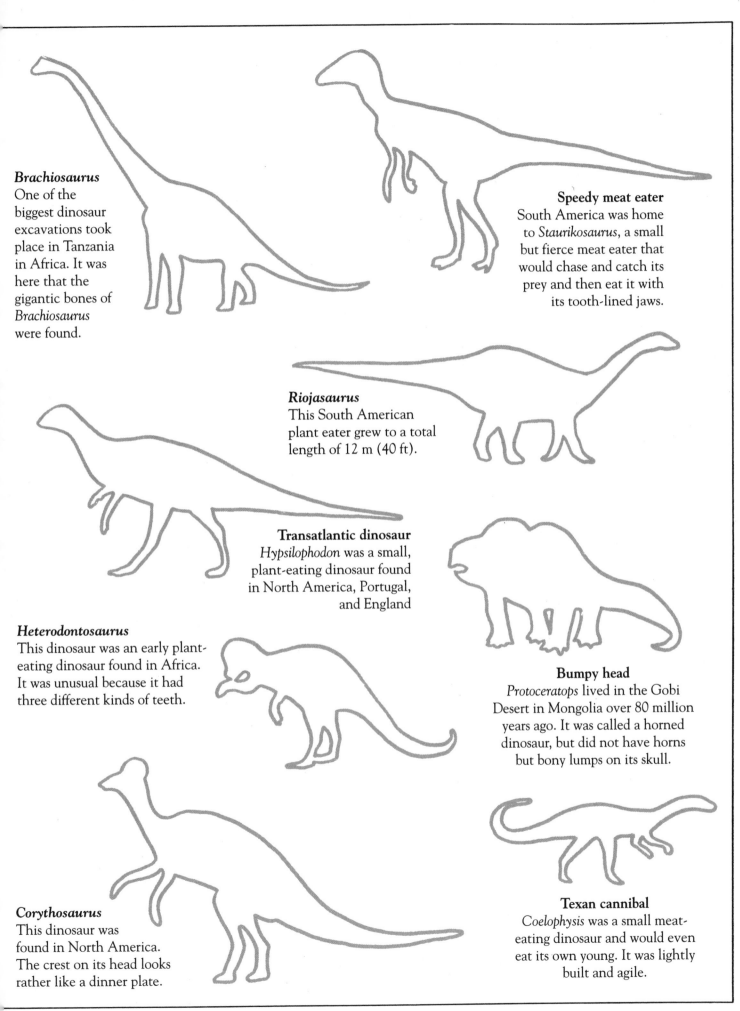

Brachiosaurus
One of the biggest dinosaur excavations took place in Tanzania in Africa. It was here that the gigantic bones of *Brachiosaurus* were found.

Speedy meat eater
South America was home to *Staurikosaurus*, a small but fierce meat eater that would chase and catch its prey and then eat it with its tooth-lined jaws.

Riojasaurus
This South American plant eater grew to a total length of 12 m (40 ft).

Transatlantic dinosaur
Hypsilophodon was a small, plant-eating dinosaur found in North America, Portugal, and England

Heterodontosaurus
This dinosaur was an early plant-eating dinosaur found in Africa. It was unusual because it had three different kinds of teeth.

Bumpy head
Protoceratops lived in the Gobi Desert in Mongolia over 80 million years ago. It was called a horned dinosaur, but did not have horns but bony lumps on its skull.

Corythosaurus
This dinosaur was found in North America. The crest on its head looks rather like a dinner plate.

Texan cannibal
Coelophysis was a small meat-eating dinosaur and would even eat its own young. It was lightly built and agile.

Tallest and smallest

Not all dinosaurs were giants. Some were as small as cats. The biggest dinosaurs ever were the plant-eating sauropods which could grow as big as a four-storey building. The smallest dinosaurs were often crafty meat eaters.

Giant turtle
At almost 4 m (14 ft) long, *Archelon* is one of the biggest turtles ever to have lived on Earth.

Meat-eating monster
Tyrannosaurus rex was the fiercest dinosaur. It had huge jaws, and lots of long, sharp teeth. It was taller than a double decker bus and 14 m (46 ft) long.

Long tail
Diplodocus had a long neck and an even longer tail and was one of the biggest dinosaurs that ever lived.

Heavy-headed giant
With its three horns and big bony frill, *Triceratops* must have had one of the heaviest heads of all time.

Armoured giant
Stegosaurus was the biggest plated dinosaur. As well as bony armour, it had two pairs of dangerous spikes at the end of its tail.

Bactrosaurus
At only 4 m (13 ft) long, this was the smallest of the duck-billed dinosaurs.

Long neck
The longest neck of all time belonged to *Mamenchisaurus*. It was three times as long as a giraffe's neck and stretched to almost 15 m (51 ft).

PONIES

Riding ponies

All ponies can be ridden, but some breeds have characteristics that make them more suitable than others. Versatility is most important, so that the pony can be used for trekking, jumping, or hunting. The hardiness and sure-footedness found in mountain ponies needs to be combined with courage, intelligence, and a natural jumping ability. A calm and predictable temperament is also useful, since ponies are primarily ridden by children. These qualities can occur naturally, but some ponies are specially bred to produce them.

Head protector
A hard hat is covered with velvet and has a peak at the front. It should always be worn to protect the head.

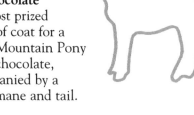

Hot chocolate
The most prized colour of coat for a Rocky Mountain Pony is rich chocolate, accompanied by a flaxen mane and tail.

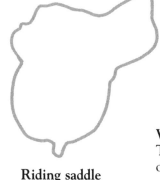

Riding saddle
A saddle should be comfortable for both horse and rider. The underside has padded panels to keep pressure off the horse's spine.

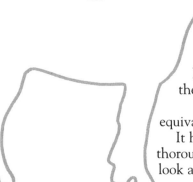

Wild West style
The leather parts of this Mexican-style saddle are skilfully engraved. The buckles, studs, and stirrups are all heavily decorated.

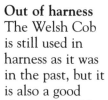

Out of harness
The Welsh Cob is still used in harness as it was in the past, but it is also a good choice for trekking.

Special cross
Developed specially for the show ring, the Riding Pony is the juvenile equivalent of the show hack. It has the proportions of a thoroughbred, but retains the look and character of a pony.

Scottish born
Originally from the Scottish Highlands, this versatile pony is very strong and has a docile temperament.

Riding position
Once astride your pony, sit upright in the middle of the saddle, holding the reins in both hands. Keep your head up, your elbows close to your sides, and your heels down.

Old favourite
The Exmoor from southwest
England is the oldest British
mountain and moorland breed. Its
coat can be a bay, brown, or dun
colour with black points.

Austrian beauty
The Haflinger is reared on
the high alpine pastures of the
Austrian Tyrol. Its palomino
colouring and flaxen mane
and tail are very striking.

Wooden horse
The Sandalwood is named
after the wood that is exported
from the islands of Sumba and
Sumbawa in Indonesia,
where it comes from.

Spanish steed
The Galiceno from Mexico
descends from Spanish stock. Its
size makes it a good in-between
mount for riders making the
change from ponies to horses.

Head gear
The bridle fits on the
pony's head and keeps
the bit in place in its
mouth. This one has a
jointed snaffle bit.

Once wild
The Landais used to live semi-wild
in the wooded region of southwest
France. It has a light build, but is
hardy and easy to keep, making it
an ideal pony for children.

Leg wear
Buff-coloured
jodhpurs let
the legs bend
more easily.
Leather boots
with silver
spurs are
worn on
special days.

Indonesian export
Ponies of Timor are hardy
and versatile. They are
sold to Australia where
they are considered to be
good riding ponies.

Arabian cross
Originally from
Sumatra, the
Padang was bred
by crossing local
stock with Arabian
blood to produce
a pony of quality.

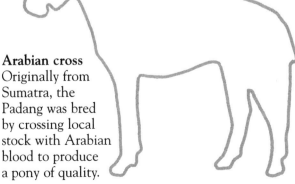

Working ponies

In the past, the native ponies of northern Europe were used as pack animals and for work in coal mines and on farms. Today, horsepower is no longer widely used in Europe and North America, but in many developing countries ponies are still kept to work under harness and to carry heavy loads. The ponies used need to be strong, hardy, and able to survive on very little food in a harsh environment.

Living underground
The Shetland was often used for work in underground coal mines. It had a hard life in the cold, wet, dark tunnels of the pits.

Italian mountain breed
The Bardigiano from the Appenines in Italy is a strong pony of great character. Hardy, quick-moving, and sure-footed, it is well-suited to all kinds of mountain work.

Good all-rounder
In spite of its name, the Icelandic Horse is a pony. It is used for all types of work in Iceland and can carry grown men without tiring.

Farm worker
The Huçul is a prime example of a working pony. It is principally used under harness for light agricultural work in the farming communities of Poland.

Hardy Greek
The Skyrian is known to be good-tempered and to jump well. It is strong and has great stamina, making it a popular working pony.

Strong by nature
The sturdy Dales was originally used as a pack animal in the mining communities of northern England. Today, its natural strength and calm temperament make it an ideal riding pony.

Curly covering
Bashkirs need to be very tough to survive the freezing temperatures of the Russian Steppes. In winter, this chestnut pony grows a thick, curly coat.

Small but mighty
Shetlands were first bred as farm animals. Despite their very small size, they can quite easily pull a heavily-loaded cart of hay.

Black beast
The Ariégeois is most at home in conditions of snow and ice. As a pack pony it can work well on steep and icy mountain tracks.

Alpine tractor
The powerful Fjord takes the place of the tractor on mountain farms. It can pull a plough and carry loads over steep tracks.

Bashkir
The Bashkir is one of the strongest ponies. It is used as a pack animal and can pull a sleigh long distances without needing food.

Indonesian taxi
The principal use of the Java is for drawing taxi carts in the towns. These provide a system of transport for both people and provisions.

Brilliant action
The fine, high-stepping action, combined with an intelligent pony character, makes the Hackney Pony most spectacular in harness.

Batak
The Batak has a reputation for being docile and good-natured. It is used for all kinds of work.

21

Ponies for sport

There are all kinds of sports for a rider to enjoy. Mounted games, or gymkhanas are great fun and can improve the young rider's balance, confidence, and skill. At these shows there are also jumping competitions to suit all age groups. An experienced rider can take part in more difficult activities such as dressage, eventing, or polo. A serious competitor will need a pony that performs well in their chosen event, so many ponies today are specially bred to succeed in the show ring.

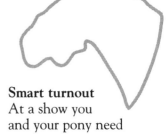

Smart turnout
At a show you and your pony need to look smart. A plaited mane may take a lot of practice to perfect, but the final effect is worth it.

Bred for harness
The American Shetland was bred by crossing the Shetland with the Hackney. It is a smart harness pony which performs well in all driving competitions.

Colourful combinations
Eventing is one of the most demanding sports in which a horse and rider can compete. Three days are spent taking part in dressage, cross-country, and showjumping events to test the pair to their limits.

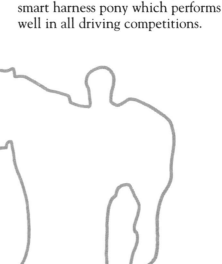

After the show
A pony will be tired and dirty after a competition. Mud and sweat should be wiped off with a sponge to make the coat shiny and glossy again.

Hockey on horseback
Polo originated in Argentina. The object of the game is to score goals by hitting a willow ball through two goal posts. The polo stick is made of bamboo. Gloves are worn to give riders a good grip.

Irish champion
A brilliant performance pony, the Connemara is fast, courageous, and a superb jumper. Its native Irish origins have given the pony a natural hardiness and endurance.

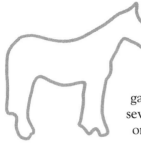

Fast and nimble
Specially trained Polo Ponies can stop, start, turn, and sprint very quickly. The game is very tiring for them, so several ponies may be ridden by one rider during a single game.

No longer wild
Few Dartmoors are found in the wild today. It is a brilliant riding pony with great jumping ability, and is now widely bred to be used in competitions.

Fun for everyone
There are many events to compete in at a gymkhana. In the egg and spoon race, you have to lead your pony with one hand, and hold an egg and spoon in the other.

Winning a prize
Coming first in a competition is very exciting for the young rider. But if you win a prize, remember to thank your pony. After all, the pony does do most of the hard work.

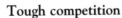

Tough competition
There are four players in a polo team. They play at a gallop, trying to score as many goals as possible, in up to six periods of seven and a half minutes.

Sure and strong
The sure-footed Pindos Pony from Greece used to be used as a pack pony. Its natural strength makes it an ideal riding and driving pony.

Show pony
The elegant Welsh Pony has been bred to perform in the show ring. The combination of its natural hardiness, together with a fine bone structure produce a winning team.

Harness racing
Trotting races are carried out over a distance of 1.5 km (1 mile). It is a modern-day form of the chariot race.

Wild ponies

There are no longer any truly wild ponies, but all over the world there are many herds of ponies living in a wild state. All the same, many ponies today retain characteristics from their ancestors that helped them to survive in the wild. The natural environment they lived in has influenced their size, the type of coat they have, and the sturdiness of their limbs.

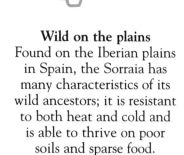

Wild on the plains
Found on the Iberian plains in Spain, the Sorraia has many characteristics of its wild ancestors; it is resistant to both heat and cold and is able to thrive on poor soils and sparse food.

Still running wild
Herds of ponies have lived in the New Forest woodlands of southern England for centuries. Today, some still do run wild, but many are reared on stud farms since they make ideal riding ponies.

Small and strong
The original habitat of the smallest British pony is the bleak and windy Shetland Islands off the northeast coast of Scotland. An inhospitable environment has made it hardy; it has stocky limbs and a thick coat.

Moor-dwelling ponies
Many Fell ponies live wild on the moors in northern England. Although they are in fact owned, they are left to live and breed with very little human interference.

Konik
Widespread in Poland, the Konik retains much of the hardiness of its wild Tarpan ancestors.

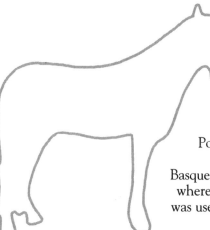

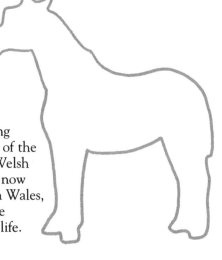

Pottock
The semi-wild Pottock is native to the mountainous Basque region of France, where for many years it was used as a pack pony.

Welsh beauty
Recognized as being the most beautiful of the pony breeds, the Welsh Mountain Pony is now widely bred. Yet in Wales, it remains a unique feature of country life.

PUPPIES

Playing and learning

Puppies are constantly alert and need exercise and play to keep them happy and active. Playing games helps a puppy to bond with its litter or its owner, and stops it becoming destructive. It is also how a puppy learns about balance and coordination. Puppies have a natural desire to search and chase, and will play energetically, exercising their growing limbs.

Scent clues
Once a puppy's senses have developed, they become very curious. They explore their surroundings, and begin to learn about the smells other animals leave behind.

Enough is enough
Energetic play is part of every healthy young dog's life. Sleep is also important, and these puppies have worn themselves out. Dogs often sleep with their backs against something comforting or protective.

Touch move
Newborn puppies use scent and heat to find their mothers. Within three weeks, other senses take over, and the touch sensors on their paws have developed to help them explore.

Balancing act
When a puppy finds a new toy, it will touch and pat it before tasting it. This means standing on one front paw, which helps to develop the puppy's balance.

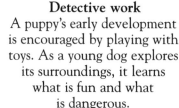

Detective work
A puppy's early development is encouraged by playing with toys. As a young dog explores its surroundings, it learns what is fun and what is dangerous.

Contact sport
Making contact with other puppies is a vital part of play. Dogs use their body movements to communicate, and learning how to understand these signals is very important.

Bowing down
This is the position that dogs use to show they are not being aggressive, that they are friendly. Puppies use this position when they play, asking other dogs to join in their games.

Attention seeking
Puppies are natural pack animals, and therefore need attention and company. Being held by its owner makes this puppy feel safe and happy, and being stroked relaxes it.

Fearless fighters
When they are young, puppies don't understand fear. They will play-fight with other puppies regardless of their size and strength. At about eight weeks they develop more cautious behaviour, and become careful when play-fighting.

Friend or foe
When a puppy first meets an older dog, it learns about social behaviour. If the dog is friendly, the puppy learns that they can play without needing to fight.

Playing safe
It is important that puppies have their own toys to play with, otherwise they will help themselves to yours. Plastic or rubber toys are safer than sticks and stones.

Leader of the pack
Once a puppy has left its mother, its owner becomes the new pack leader. A puppy will rely on its owner to play with it and provide food and exercise. Puppies can become destructive without exercise.

Good enough to eat
This puppy is bowing to its toy, showing that it is excited and ready to play. The senses of smell and taste are the first ones used by puppies when exploring new objects.

Dog-napping
Although puppies need more sleep, all dogs doze throughout the day. Yawning usually means they are about to settle down, and shows they are totally relaxed.

Biting back
It is natural pack behaviour for puppies to bite when they play. They learn about their own strength and how other puppies will react to them if they are aggressive.

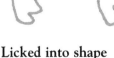

Licked into shape
Grooming is one of the things that puppies learn from their mother. While they are young, they often copy her behaviour and practise grooming each other.

Keeping guard
Puppies naturally guard and protect their toys, food, and even their owners. They may show aggression if they feel threatened by other puppies.

Various breeds

All domestic puppies are related to the Grey Wolf. There are over 400 types of pedigree dog, most of which have developed from working dogs. There are also many cross-breed dogs. Each breed has certain characteristics which makes it different from other dogs, such as better sight, smell, or strength. Most puppies are the same size when they are young, regardless of their breed, and they can look quite different from their parents.

Fiery red-head
The Spaniel developed in Britain as a hunting dog. Spaniels that are one colour can have a more aggressive nature than mixed coloured varieties.

Black beauty
The Labrador Retriever is one of the most intelligent, loyal and responsive breeds. They are very good with children, and make reliable family pets.

Mistaken identity
The Great Dane was developed in Germany, and was used to guard castles. The puppies are born with adult sized feet, and look quite clumsy until their bodies have caught up.

Father and son
The Caucasian Sheepdog was developed to herd and protect sheep on the harsh mountains of the former USSR. It is tall and strong, and has a thick, warm coat.

Bundle of gold
This Golden Retriever puppy is only one week old. It looks very different from its mother now, but in six months its coat and markings will be fully developed.

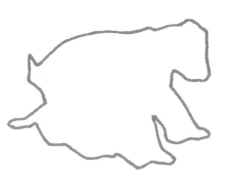

Tiny terror
Jack Russell Terriers are small, lively puppies, growing only to about 35 cm (14 in) tall. They can have either brown, black, or orange markings.

Giant eaters
Great Dane puppies are friendly, tolerant, and gentle. They make excellent family pets, if you can afford the huge food bills.

Puppy fat
Shar Pei puppies are covered in big folds of skin, which are still visible when they are adult. It makes them look sad, but in fact they are calm, gentle, and independent dogs.

Mixed bunch
There are many more cross-breed puppies than any pedigree breed. It is often claimed that they make healthier and friendlier family pets.

Powerful pair
This Canary puppy is sitting with its powerful father. Like the Shar Pei, Canary dogs have loose, wrinkly skin. The puppies are determined and strong.

Mountain climbers
These stocky puppies are strong mountain dogs. The black puppy is a Bernese Mountain Dog. In the past, they were used in Switzerland to pull carts carrying market produce.

Scots guard
West Highland White Terrier puppies are not much smaller than their tiny parents. They are affectionate and lively puppies. Surprisingly, "Westies" also make excellent guard dogs.

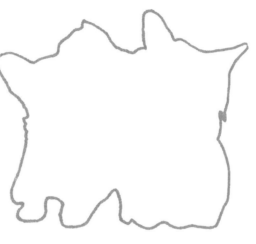

Pale imitation
This small fluffy puppy will grow into a strong Australian Cattle Dog. Its coat will get much darker, and the markings more obvious. The white colouring comes from Dalmatian blood in its ancestry.

Unique pet
This puppy is a cross-breed. Its mother and father are from different breeds, and it has characteristics of both parents.

Veiled Terrier
These Skye Terriers have beautiful long coats that need regular grooming to stay clean and shiny. The hair on their heads is shorter, but when the puppies get older it will form a curtain over their eyes.

Family favourite
The colour of the Golden Retriever's coat is one reason why it is among the most popular choices for a pet. It is an easy puppy to train, and enjoys family life as long as it gets plenty of exercise.

Sleepy Spaniel
Cocker Spaniels are active and playful puppies. They show their excitement by wagging their tails furiously. After racing around this puppy is ready for a doze.

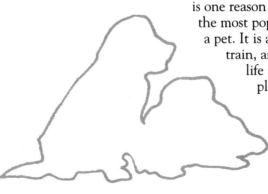

Puppy care

 Puppies have many of the same instincts as humans. Like humans, they enjoy friendship and prefer living in a pack, either with their litter, or with a human family. A puppy will be old enough to leave its litter at about nine weeks. It is important to train a puppy while still young so that it will fit happily into your home.

Travelling light
Puppies often have to visit the vet during the first few months of their lives, and a safe, secure travel box is the easiest way to get there.

Brotherly love
It is very important that puppies develop friendships while they are young, so that they learn to communicate. It will help them grow into friendly, confident dogs.

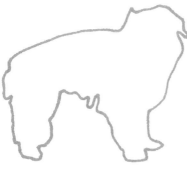

Dry cleaning
Giving this puppy a regular brush will keep its coat shiny and clean. It also gives its owner a chance to check for health problems and hair loss.

Three's a crowd
By five weeks, puppies are no longer entirely dependant on their mother. All their senses are fully developed, and they start to become curious. Soon they won't need each other and will happily explore alone.

Body language
You can tell that this puppy is happy because its tail is raised and wagging, and its ears are in a relaxed position. Puppies give us very clear signs to tell us how they are feeling.

Collar practise
Puppies should start to wear a collar from six weeks, but only for a short time each day until they are used to it. The size of the collar must be checked regularly as the puppy grows.

Comfort food
These six-week-old puppies don't need their mother's milk any more. She allows them to feed though, because it is comforting for both her and her growing litter.

A helping hand
While a puppy is young, its owner acts as its mother. Grooming a puppy helps you to become friends, and keeps it clean at the same time.

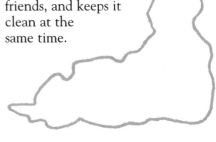

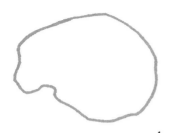

A dog's life
Young puppies spend most of their time either feeding or sleeping. Puppies will play energetically and become very excited in short bursts, and then sleep heavily. This is normal in a healthy puppy.

Bed time
Puppies are very sociable and enjoy being with people even when they are tired, so the best place for a puppy's bed is in a busy part of the house. It is best not to buy a hard bed for your puppy until it has stopped teething.

Dining alone
As a puppy gets older, its natural instinct is to protect its food from other dogs, as it would have done in the wild. It may growl if you get close, so it is best to let a puppy eat alone.

Soft touch
Puppies are comforted by attention and touch. This young puppy is happy to be fed by its new owner, and they will become friends through this contact.

Taking a walk
As a puppy grows, it needs more space to exercise. While they are still young, puppies should be taught to walk on a lead without getting either nervous or over-excited.

Helpless bundles
As soon as all her puppies are born, the mother cleans them and lets them feed. These puppies are almost totally helpless without her at this age.

All grown up
Puppies are all born roughly the same size regardless of how big they may grow. It is important to choose a dog that won't grow too big for your house, or need more exercise than you can give it.

Tricks of the trade
These puppies are looking up pleadingly, hoping for food or attention. They learned to do this with their mothers, and now show the same behaviour with their owner.

Mother's pride
This mother is relaxing with her young litter. Her puppies have learned how to feed and, whilst they are small, it is a pleasurable activity for her.

Puppies in training

Not all puppies are pets. Some puppies are chosen to be trained for work when they are adult. For instance they may become farm dogs, racing dogs, or hunting dogs.

Puppies are chosen because of certain qualities in their breed, such as strength, speed, or responsiveness.

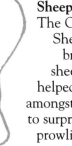

Sheep's clothing
The Old English Sheepdog was bred to herd sheep. Its coat helped it to hide amongst the sheep to surprise hungry, prowling wolves.

Versatile puppies
Labrador puppies are used for many different types of work, including hunting. Originally from Canada, they used to help fishermen to drag their nets ashore.

Worth their weight in gold
Golden Retriever puppies are often chosen to be trained as guide dogs for blind owners. They are easy to train, and make excellent companions.

Australian Cattle Dogs
Originally used to herd cattle in Australia, these puppies have thick coats, strong backs, and muscular legs. They are well behaved and hard workers.

Gentle gundog
The Spaniel has a long, wide nose for smelling, and a gentle, delicate bite, making it the ideal puppy for tracking and retrieving game.

A little terrier
The Yorkshire Terrier was bred by miners to hunt for rats in the coal pits. The puppies are playful and intelligent.

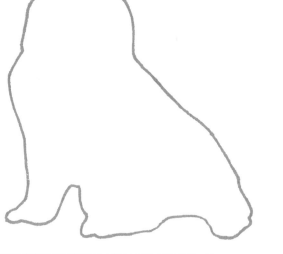

Friendly giant
This strong St. Bernard puppy was originally bred to search for and rescue people lost on mountains in Switzerland.

Elegant companions
Italian Greyhounds were historically kept as ladies' companions because they are quiet and friendly. Larger Greyhounds are used as racing dogs.

ANIMALS

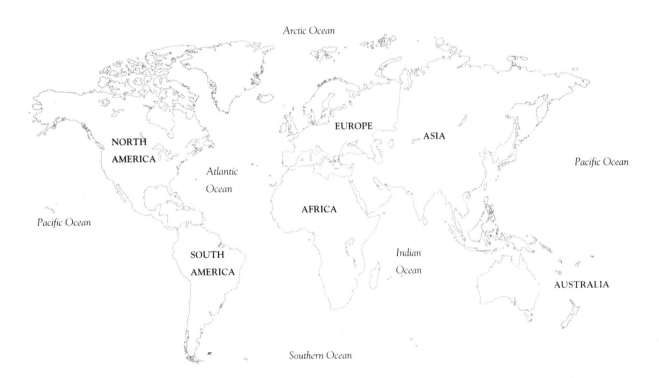

Arctic Ocean

NORTH
AMERICA

EUROPE

ASIA

Pacific Ocean

Atlantic
Ocean

Pacific Ocean

AFRICA

SOUTH
AMERICA

Indian
Ocean

AUSTRALIA

Southern Ocean

Africa

Deserts, grasslands, and tropical jungles make up the vast continent of Africa, home to some of the world's most beautiful animals. However, many of them are hunted for their skins or tusks, and are in danger of becoming extinct.

Sensitive pig
The bush pig, or wild boar, uses its long, sensitive snout to sniff out roots, insects, and worms. They are often hunted by farmers because they damage crops.

Sand shoes
With thick fur under its feet, the sand cat is protected from scorching hot sand. Its broad, furry paws stop it from sinking into the soft sand.

Handyman
The chimpanzee is one of the few animals that makes tools. It uses a stone as a hammer, for example.

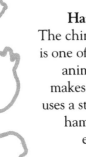

Like mother, like daughter
A herd of elephants usually consists of female elephants, called cows, and their offspring, led by the oldest cow. When young males reach maturity, they leave the herd to live alone.

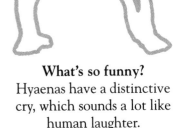

What's so funny?
Hyaenas have a distinctive cry, which sounds a lot like human laughter.

Top cat
A thick mane, proud bearing, and fearful roar have made the lion "king of the beasts".

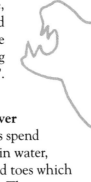

Down by the river
Hippopotamuses spend most of the day in water, and have webbed toes which help them swim. They can stay underwater for up to six minutes.

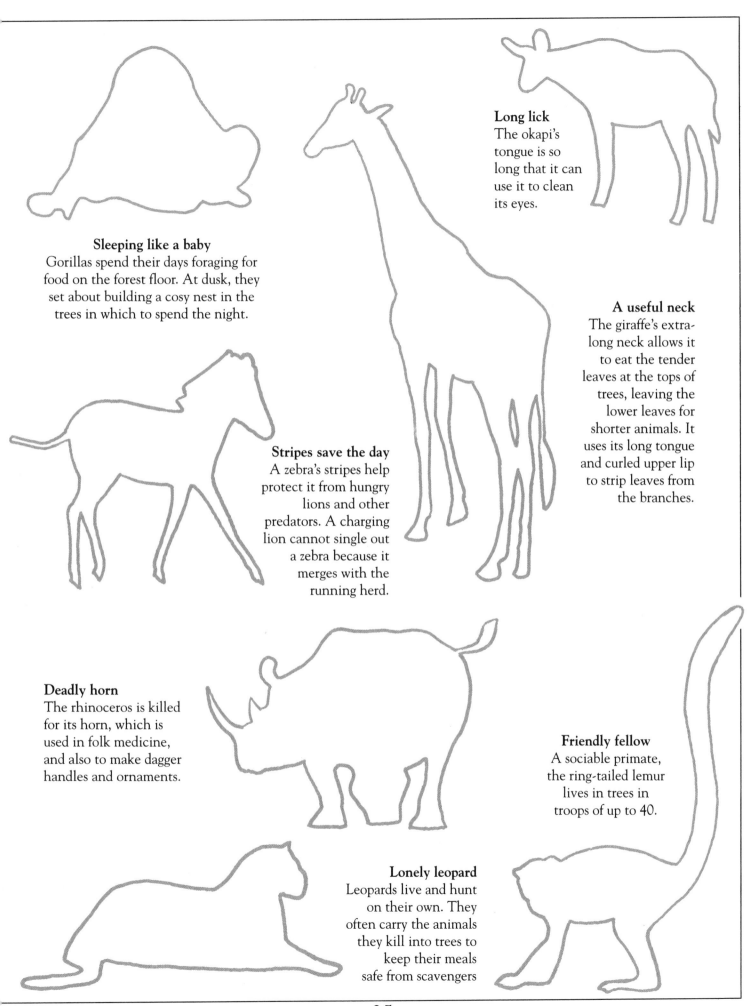

Long lick
The okapi's tongue is so long that it can use it to clean its eyes.

Sleeping like a baby
Gorillas spend their days foraging for food on the forest floor. At dusk, they set about building a cosy nest in the trees in which to spend the night.

A useful neck
The giraffe's extra-long neck allows it to eat the tender leaves at the tops of trees, leaving the lower leaves for shorter animals. It uses its long tongue and curled upper lip to strip leaves from the branches.

Stripes save the day
A zebra's stripes help protect it from hungry lions and other predators. A charging lion cannot single out a zebra because it merges with the running herd.

Deadly horn
The rhinoceros is killed for its horn, which is used in folk medicine, and also to make dagger handles and ornaments.

Friendly fellow
A sociable primate, the ring-tailed lemur lives in trees in troops of up to 40.

Lonely leopard
Leopards live and hunt on their own. They often carry the animals they kill into trees to keep their meals safe from scavengers

Asia

God of the Monkeys
The graceful Hanuman langur is named after the Hindu monkey god. It is a sacred animal in India.

No continent equals Asia in size or in variety of natural features. Asia has some of the world's highest mountains, longest rivers, largest deserts and plains, and thickest forests and jungles. The highest and lowest places on Earth are in Asia.

Wild about horns
The markhor is a wild goat. Its huge curly horns may grow up to 1.1 m (4 ft) long.

A delicate nose
The Malayan tapir has a short sensitive trunk, which helps it pull leaves and shoots into its mouth.

Clean living
Red pandas often wash themselves like a cat, licking a foot and then wiping the wet foot over their fur.

Furball
Pallas's cat has a very long and thick coat, much longer than other wild cats. It is thought to be an ancestor of domestic long-haired cats.

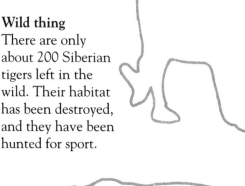

Wild thing
There are only about 200 Siberian tigers left in the wild. Their habitat has been destroyed, and they have been hunted for sport.

The giant raccoon?
Each giant panda lives alone in its own terrritory in the misty mountain forests of south-west China. When it was first discovered in 1869, scientists thought it was a big raccoon.

Long-armed monkey
The orang-utan has long, muscular arms which reach down to its ankles. It uses them to swing through the trees.

Australia

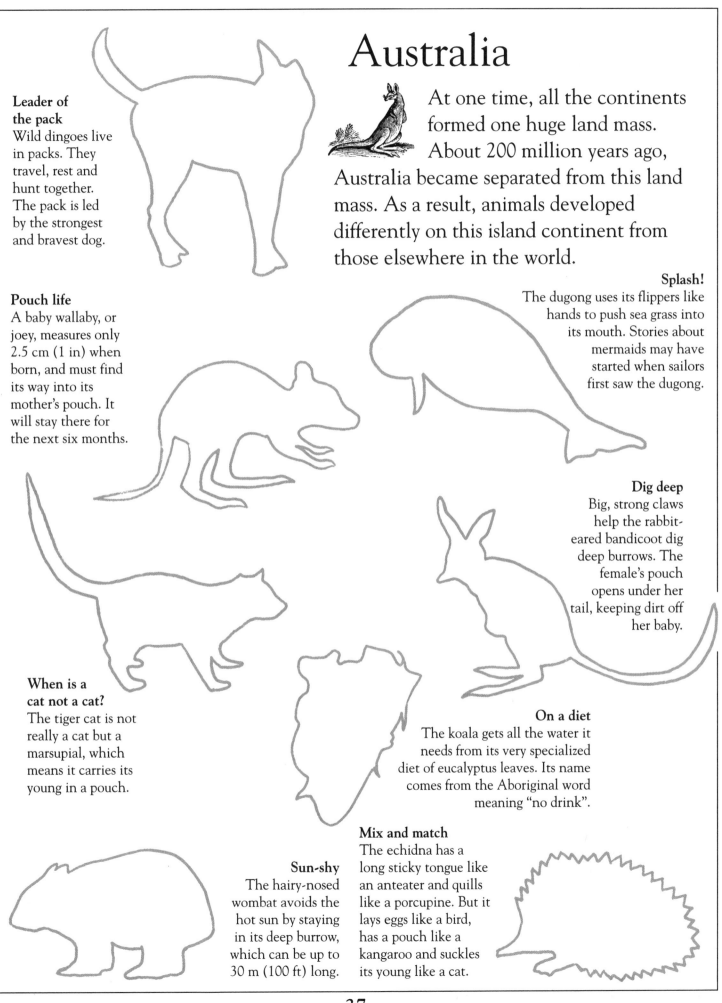

At one time, all the continents formed one huge land mass. About 200 million years ago, Australia became separated from this land mass. As a result, animals developed differently on this island continent from those elsewhere in the world.

Leader of the pack
Wild dingoes live in packs. They travel, rest and hunt together. The pack is led by the strongest and bravest dog.

Pouch life
A baby wallaby, or joey, measures only 2.5 cm (1 in) when born, and must find its way into its mother's pouch. It will stay there for the next six months.

Splash!
The dugong uses its flippers like hands to push sea grass into its mouth. Stories about mermaids may have started when sailors first saw the dugong.

Dig deep
Big, strong claws help the rabbit-eared bandicoot dig deep burrows. The female's pouch opens under her tail, keeping dirt off her baby.

When is a cat not a cat?
The tiger cat is not really a cat but a marsupial, which means it carries its young in a pouch.

On a diet
The koala gets all the water it needs from its very specialized diet of eucalyptus leaves. Its name comes from the Aboriginal word meaning "no drink".

Sun-shy
The hairy-nosed wombat avoids the hot sun by staying in its deep burrow, which can be up to 30 m (100 ft) long.

Mix and match
The echidna has a long sticky tongue like an anteater and quills like a porcupine. But it lays eggs like a bird, has a pouch like a kangaroo and suckles its young like a cat.

The Americas

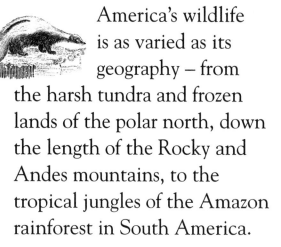

America's wildlife is as varied as its geography – from the harsh tundra and frozen lands of the polar north, down the length of the Rocky and Andes mountains, to the tropical jungles of the Amazon rainforest in South America.

Santa's big helper
The reindeer, or caribou, is the only species of deer where both males and females have antlers.

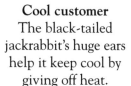

Cool customer
The black-tailed jackrabbit's huge ears help it keep cool by giving off heat.

Killer Tongue
Anteaters use their claws to tear open nests, and they lick up ants and termites with their long sticky tongues.

Warm fur coat
Many chinchillas have been killed for their thick fur, which is used to make fur coats and jackets.

Golden fleece
The alpaca has a long, shaggy coat of fine, soft hair. Alpacas are shorn like sheep and their fleece is used to make yarn for clothes.

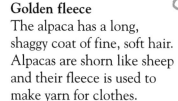

Lethal weapons
During the autumn breeding season, male wapitis fight each other with their huge antlers to compete for a mate.

Deer little thing
The smallest deer is only 40 cm (15 in) high. But because the pudu is so shy, not much is known about it.

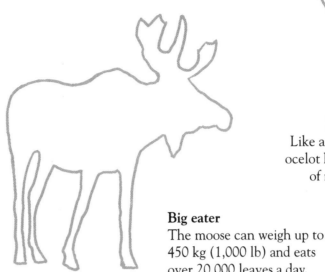

Individual prints
Like a set of fingerprints, each ocelot has an individual pattern of markings on its coat.

Bows and arrows
When threatened, the porcupine bows its back, raises its quills and lashes its tail. Its tail quills are barbed, like an arrow.

Big eater
The moose can weigh up to 450 kg (1,000 lb) and eats over 20,000 leaves a day.

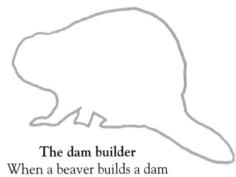

"Little armoured one"
When Spanish soldiers invaded South America in the 16th century, they found a very odd-looking animal. They called it the armadillo, which means "little armoured one".

The dam builder
When a beaver builds a dam across a river, a pond is formed. The pond provides food, as well as the sticks and mud which beavers use to build their lodges.

Spot the difference
Unlike the leopard, the jaguar has black marks inside each ring of spots.

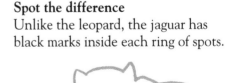

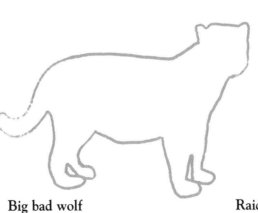

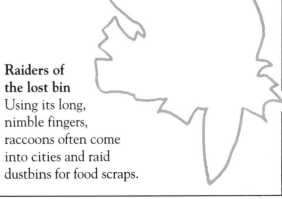

Big bad wolf
If a maned wolf is threatened, the mane of hair on its neck and shoulders stands up to make it look bigger and more frightening.

Raiders of the lost bin
Using its long, nimble fingers, raccoons often come into cities and raid dustbins for food scraps.

Europe

Europe is the most densely populated and industrialized continent in the world. Most of Europe's wild animals therefore live in remote, hard-to-reach areas, or in zoos and national parks.

Spot the hunter
Keen eyesight, smell, and hearing make the spotted genet one of the most efficient hunters in the civet family.

A sure thing
The sure-footed chamois has an incredible sense of balance. It can keep its footing on rocks no bigger than the palm of a human hand.

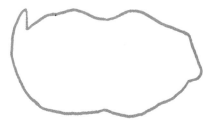

A sett of badgers
Badgers live in burrows called setts. When digging, badgers can close their ears and nostrils to keep out the dirt.

Velvet skin
Newly grown antlers are covered in a protective skin called velvet. Male fallow deers grow new antlers every year.

Excellent ears
The long tufts on its ears are thought to help the rare Spanish lynx hear well.

Bear-ly awake
In autumn, the brown bear fattens up on roots, shoots, fruits, and berries to last it through the winter, when it hibernates.

Bright-eyed and bushy-tailed
The red squirrel uses its long, bushy tail for balance. It usually climbs down a tree head first.

Missing from the Mediterranean
The beaches where the Mediterranean monk seal used to breed have been taken over by holidaymakers.

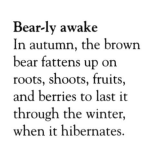

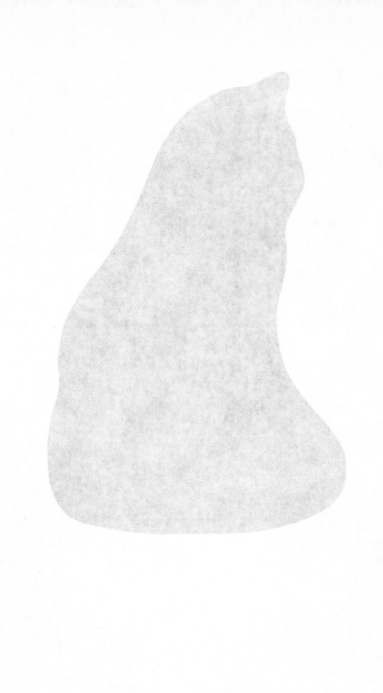

IN THE RED

Non-pedigree
marmalade
shorthair

Red
Burmese

Marmalade
alley cat

British
cream
shorthair

Pedigree red
tabby shorthair

Non-pedigree
marmalade alley
cat with white
socks and bib

Beautiful
green gaze

Good buddies!

Ten-week-old red
Burmese kittens

Red self
longhair

Cat napping

TABBIES

Exotic
shorthair

Non-pedigree
tabby longhair

Chocolate
tabby angora

Sleepy
tabby

Non-
pedigree
tabby

Grooming each other

Stretching and
rolling

Chocolate
tabby-point
Siamese

Non-pedigree tabby longhair

Shorthair
tabby kitten

Blue classic tabby
longhair

Tabby
kitten

Exotic
shorthair

BLACK

Black-and-white
non-pedigree farm cat

Lively and
curious at
only ten
weeks old

Back off!

Non-pedigree
shorthair

British black shorthair

Non-pedigree
longhair

Bicolour
longhair

British
black
short-
hair

Black longhair

Ten-week-
old kittens
love to play

Non-pedigree black-and-
white longhair

Green-
eyed
Bombay

Black
longhair

Best buddies

KITTENS

Tabby kitten

Black-and-white kitten

Learning to pounce

Careful grooming

Fluffy longhaired kittens

Four-month-old ginger kitten

"Cat and mouse"

Tiny Tonkinese kittens

A leaping pounce at ten weeks

Anyone for a game of football?

Keeping clean

Tortoiseshell kitten

Marmalade tabby

TORTOISESHELL

Non-pedigree tortoiseshell-and-white

Tortoiseshell shorthair

Blue tortoiseshell-and-white

Oriental tortoiseshell

Blue tortoise-shell-and-white longhair

British tortoiseshell shorthair

Tortoiseshell longhair

Tortoiseshell shorthair

Blue tortoise-shell-and-white

Tortoiseshell manx

Non-pedigree tortoiseshell shorthair

Black tortoiseshell shorthair

Tortie cameo longhair

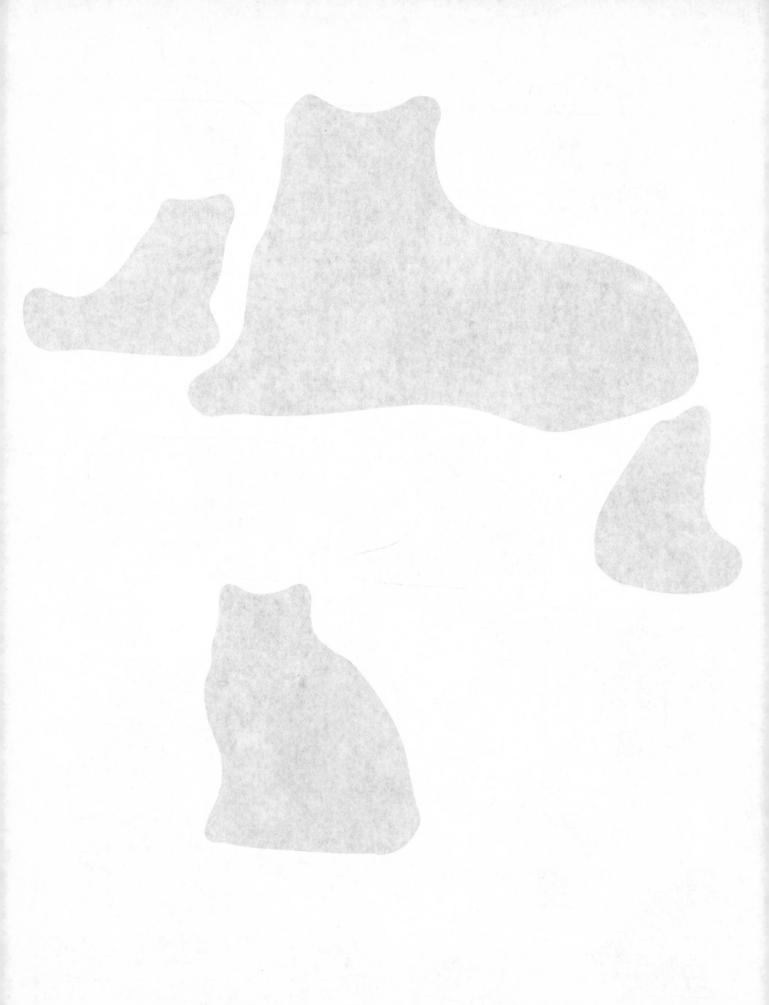

ARISTOCATS

Fluffy
colourpoint
longhair

Watchful
Siamese
kitten

Lilac-point
Siamese

Siamese kitten
washing

Burmese
buddies

Blue-point
snowshoe

Seal-point
Siamese
kitten

Lilac tabby-
point Balinese

Alert and
playful
seal-point
Siamese
kitten

Seal-point
colourpoint
ragdoll

Chocolate
Siamese
tabby-point

Foreign blue
shorthair

Seal tabby-
point
longhair

PLANT EATERS

Massospondylus' teeth were not good for grinding plants

Mamenchisaurus had a very long neck for eating leaves off tall plants

Iguanodon could walk on two feet or four

Hypsilophodon was a small dinosaur that ate low-growing plants

Diplodocus used its long neck to reach leaves high in the tree-tops

Camarasaurus was one of the longest and heaviest dinosaurs

Heterodontosaurus was only about 1 m (39 in) long

Riojasaurus walked on four legs and had a long neck and tail

Brachiosaurus stood at 12 m (39 ft) high – about as tall as a four-storey building

The bird-like *Gallimimus* had a toothless beak

HORNS AND FRILLS

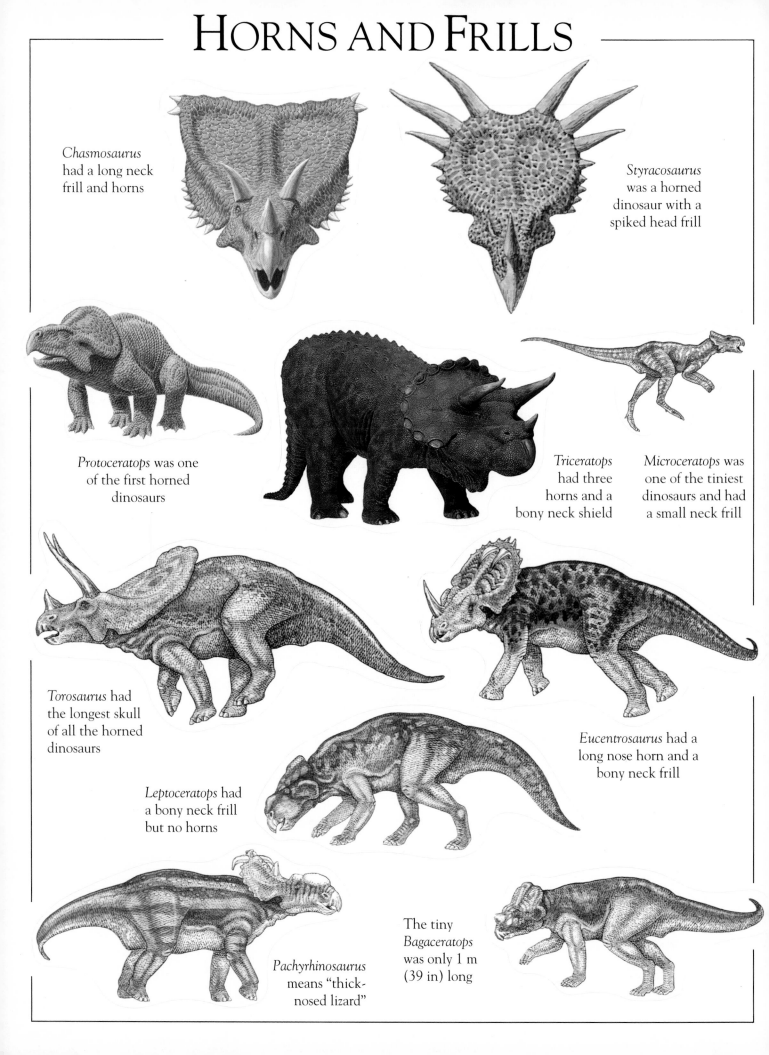

Chasmosaurus had a long neck frill and horns

Styracosaurus was a horned dinosaur with a spiked head frill

Protoceratops was one of the first horned dinosaurs

Triceratops had three horns and a bony neck shield

Microceratops was one of the tiniest dinosaurs and had a small neck frill

Torosaurus had the longest skull of all the horned dinosaurs

Eucentrosaurus had a long nose horn and a bony neck frill

Leptoceratops had a bony neck frill but no horns

Pachyrhinosaurus means "thick-nosed lizard"

The tiny *Bagaceratops* was only 1 m (39 in) long

REPTILES OF THE SEA AND AIR

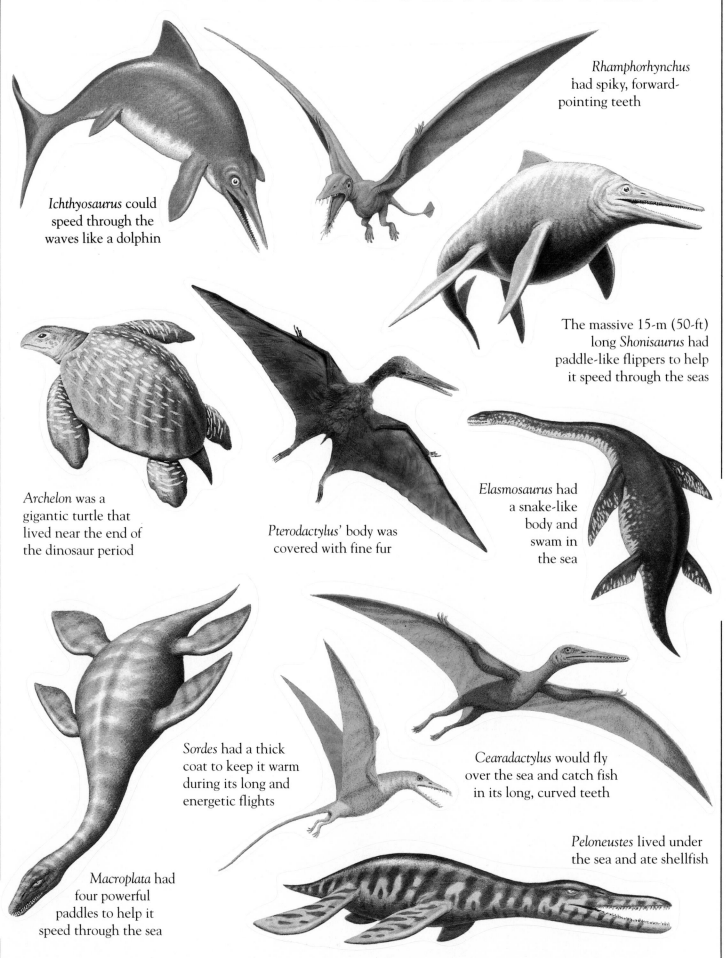

Rhamphorhynchus had spiky, forward-pointing teeth

Ichthyosaurus could speed through the waves like a dolphin

The massive 15-m (50-ft) long *Shonisaurus* had paddle-like flippers to help it speed through the seas

Archelon was a gigantic turtle that lived near the end of the dinosaur period

Pterodactylus' body was covered with fine fur

Elasmosaurus had a snake-like body and swam in the sea

Sordes had a thick coat to keep it warm during its long and energetic flights

Cearadactylus would fly over the sea and catch fish in its long, curved teeth

Peloneustes lived under the sea and ate shellfish

Macroplata had four powerful paddles to help it speed through the sea

DUCK-BILLED DINOSAURS

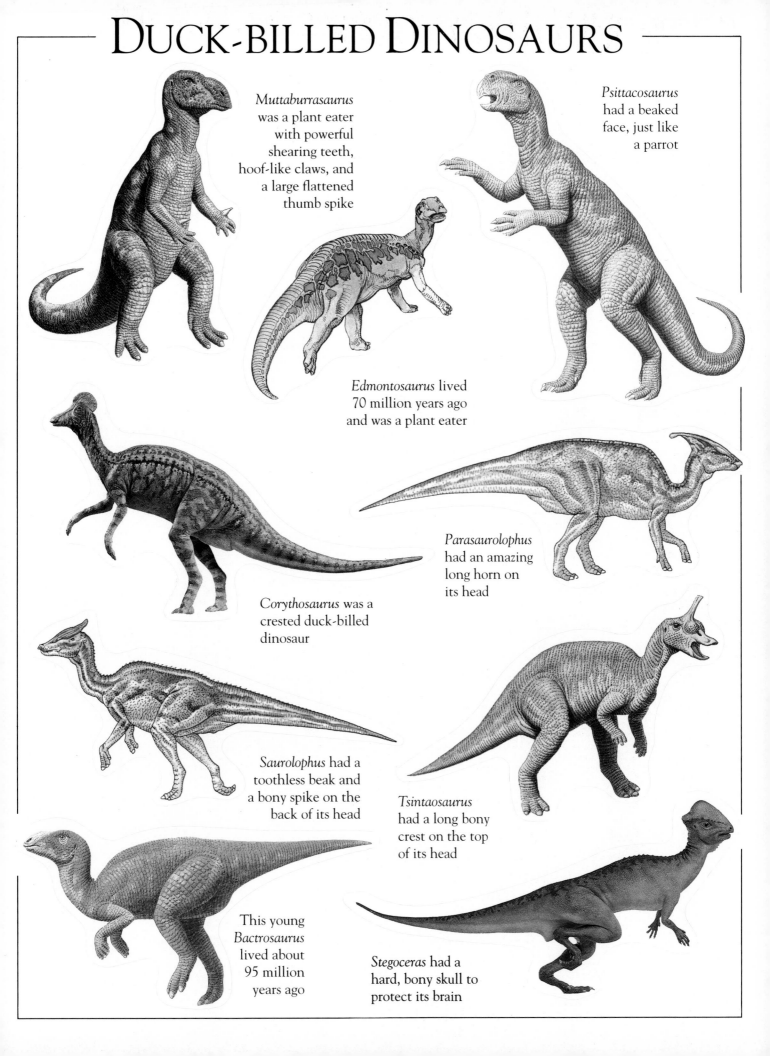

Muttaburrasaurus
was a plant eater
with powerful
shearing teeth,
hoof-like claws, and
a large flattened
thumb spike

Psittacosaurus
had a beaked
face, just like
a parrot

Edmontosaurus lived
70 million years ago
and was a plant eater

Parasaurolophus
had an amazing
long horn on
its head

Corythosaurus was a
crested duck-billed
dinosaur

Saurolophus had a
toothless beak and
a bony spike on the
back of its head

Tsintaosaurus
had a long bony
crest on the top
of its head

This young
Bactrosaurus
lived about
95 million
years ago

Stegoceras had a
hard, bony skull to
protect its brain

SPIKES AND PLATES

Polacanthus was
covered in spines

A *Stegosaurus'*
brain was only
the size of a plum

Ankylosaurs
are armoured
dinosaurs

Scelidosaurus had
armoured skin and a long
tail to help it balance

Euoplocephalus had a
huge club of bone
at the end of its
tail

Kentrosaurus had an
extra pair of spines
above its rear legs

Scolosaurus had bony
armour and two spikes
at the end of its tail

Tuojiangosaurus
had bony spikes on
the end of its tail

Pinacosaurus and
Euoplocephalus
were both
very fierce

Edmontonia was a
large, armoured
plant eater

MEAT EATERS

Deinonychus was
a fast mover and
could attack
quickly

Eustreptospondylus
had very sharp
teeth for slicing
through flesh

Velociraptor was a ferocious flesh eater
with sharp teeth and claws

Baryonyx had teeth
very similar to
those of a crocodile

Coelophysis was one of
the first dinosaurs and a
fast, two-legged runner

Herrerasaurus
lived 230 million
years ago

Ornitholestes was the smallest
meat-eating dinosaur 150
million years ago

Tyrannosaurus rex was
a giant dinosaur, as
tall as a small house

Staurikosaurus
could run fast to
catch its prey

Troödon had a big brain and
big eyes and was a good
hunter by day and night

YOU AND YOUR PONY

Champ!

Riding hat

A pony of
your own

Sponging down

Plaited mane

Riding
saddle

Hunting
jacket

Snaffle
bridle

Sitting tall

Polo
player

Gloves and
polo stick

Boots and jodhpurs

Racing cart

Western
saddle

Egg and
spoon race

Eventing colours

BRITISH AND IRISH BREEDS

Connemara

Welsh Cob

Shetland

Exmoor

Shetland

New Forest Pony

Hackney Pony

Welsh
Mountain Pony

Connemara

Dales

Dartmoor

Welsh Pony

Fell

Highland

Welsh Cob

EUROPEAN BREEDS

Konik
(Czech Republic)

Huçul
(Czech
Republic)

Haflinger
(Austria)

Icelandic Horse
(Iceland)

Bardigiano
(Italy)

Pindos Pony
(Greece)

Fjord
(Norway)

Ariégeois
(France)

Landais
(France)

Sorraia
(Spain)

Pottock
(France)

Icelandic
Horse
(Iceland)

Haflinger
(Austria)

Skyrian Horse
(Greece)

Shetland
(Britain)

PONIES OF THE WORLD

Polo Pony
(Argentina)

American
Shetland
(N. America)

Bashkir
(Russia)

Galiceno
(Mexico)

Padang
(Indonesia)

Riding Pony
(Britain)

Java
(Indonesia)

Galiceno
(Mexico)

Australian Pony

Batak
(Indonesia)

American
Shetland
(N. America)

Bashkir
(Russia)

Sandalwood
(Indonesia)

Timor
(Indonesia)

Rocky Mountain Pony
(N. America)

MAKING FRIENDS

Playful Golden
Retriever puppies

A perfect pedigree litter

Six-week-old puppies,
tired after a run

Four-week-old Great
Dane puppies

Curious puppies using
their noses

Learning to play

An older puppy
takes a look

Play-fighting Labradors

Skye Terrier puppies
with their tiny mum

Mother watching over
her sleepy litter

Making an
unusual friend

Getting a helping
hand

A litter of healthy
cross-breed puppies

A Spaniel and a Retriever
sharing a meal

This Collie is
ready for
a walk

PUPPY SHOW

A thick-coated
black puppy

A silky
red Spaniel

An Irish
Wolfhound and
his tiny pup

An Australian
Cattle Dog

A well-travelled
puppy

A Caucasian Sheepdog
puppy with its father

Old English Sheepdogs

A West Highland
White Terrier

A cuddly
St. Bernard
puppy

A playful cross-breed puppy

A sleepy Spaniel

Settling into a new home

A well-groomed
Yorkshire Terrier
puppy

Golden Retriever
playmates

Australian Cattle
Dog puppies

PUPPY SHOW

A curious Spaniel puppy

Discovering
new toys

Retrievers with
short puppy hair

A Labrador
pouncing on its toy

Young puppies
feeding from mother

A proud mum with
her pedigree litter

Teething with a
plastic bone

A Golden Retriever puppy

Two-week-old
wrinkly pup

Following the scent

Wrinkly Great
Dane giants

A Shar Pei
puppy

A Great Dane
puppy

A Spaniel
puppy

A colourful Jack
Russell

PUPPY LIFE

A healthy Terrier

Keeping your puppy clean

Graceful Italian Greyhounds

Thick-coated mountain puppies

A Canary dog with his puppy

Older puppies still trying to feed

A proud Terrier with a new collar

A Retriever puppy enjoying his meal

Watching for food

Friendly Australian Cattle Dog puppies

Fighting for attention

An exhausted young puppy

A long-legged puppy

A new partnership

The best of friends

ANIMALS IN DANGER

The blue whale is the biggest animal ever to have lived on Earth. It is even bigger than the largest known dinosaur

There are only about 300 mountain gorillas left in central Africa

The snow leopard's broad feet stop it from sinking into the snow

Today, the Spanish lynx is only found in very remote areas

The dugong is a rare sea mammal that lives in the shallow, warm coastal waters of the Indian Ocean

The Mediterranean monk seal is very rare

The Siberian tiger is the largest and rarest of all the big cats

Because people kill ocelots for their beautiful fur, the species is now very rare

Pandas are found only in very small areas of south-west China

African elephants usually live on reserves to protect them from ivory hunters

The endangered black rhinoceros used to be extremely widespread throughout Africa

Mountain Animals

Soft, thick, fur coats keep chinchillas warm high up in the Andes

The Hanuman langur lives in the forests at the foothills of the Himalayas

The pudu, the smallest deer in the world, lives in South America

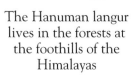

The alpaca is a relative of the camel

The chamois leaps around the rocky crags of mountainous Southern Europe

The European brown bear is short-sighted and relies on its keen sense of smell to find food

Yaks have a very long coat which reaches almost to the ground

The porcupine's coat has about 30,000 spiky quills

The wapiti gets its name from the American Indian word for "white"

The markhor's natural habitat is the woods covering the lower slopes of the Himalayan Mountains

JUNGLE ANIMALS

The three-toed sloth is the slowest animal in the Amazon jungle

The Malayan tapir is very timid and comes out mainly at night

The hairy armadillo has a suit of bony plates all over its body. It lives in South America

Hippopotamuses spend most of the day resting in lakes and rivers

The chimpanzee is extremely intelligent

The name orang-utan means "jungle man" in Malay

The okapi's nearest relative is the giraffe

The jaguar is the largest cat in South America

The branches of a leafy tree are the leopard's favourite resting spot

It is obvious how the ring-tailed lemur got its name

DESERT ANIMALS

North America is the only
place in the world you
could sniff out a skunk

Ruppell's fox lives in both
stony and sandy deserts

Australian wild
dogs, or dingoes,
are descended from
domestic dogs

The bactrian camel from
Asia has two humps, not one

Some desert tortoises from
the south-western deserts of
America are nearly 100 years old

From snowy regions to deserts,
the Australian echidna makes its
home wherever there is a supply
of juicy termites and ants

The rabbit-eared
bandicoot is an
Australian
marsupial

The sandy-coloured sand
cat is well camouflaged
in the Sahara desert

The black-tailed jackrabbit
spends the day in the
shade to escape the heat
of the American deserts

GRASSLAND ANIMALS

The hyaena's powerful jaw can crunch through hard bone

Pallas's cat lives in the harsh grasslands between China and Russia

Lions live in family groups called "prides"

The giant anteater eats up to 30,000 termites and ants daily

The Australian tiger cat is a marsupial

The wombat is a protected species in all states of Australia

Wallabies are smaller than kangaroos

The maned wolf lives on the plains of South America

Zebras live in herds of up to 200

Giraffes grow up to 5.5 m (18 ft) tall

WOODLAND ANIMALS

The spotted genet from southern Europe uses its sharp claws to cling onto tree trunks

Raccoons have fur coats to keep them warm

Koalas eat certain types of eucalyptus leaves

The European red squirrel hibernates in winter

The red panda shares the same habitat, and diet, as the giant panda

When alarmed, the bush pig raises its mane of white hair

Reindeer are also known as caribou

Although this kind of beaver is American, beavers can also be found in parts of Europe

Herds of fallow deer live in parks and woods in Europe, but as they are very shy they are rarely seen

The largest deer in the world, the moose, is found in the forests of Canada

Badgers have long front legs and sharp claws, which they use for digging

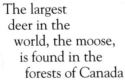

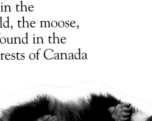